HOT COMPETITION

Marg McAlister
Illustrated by Melissa Webb

Cuisenaire
800-445-5985 www.etacuisenaire.com

Hot Competition

ISBN 0-7406-1203-4
ETA 620031

ETA/Cuisenaire • Vernon Hills, IL 60061-1862
800-445-5985 • www.etacuisenaire.com

Published by ETA/Cuisenaire® under license from
Rigby Heinemann, a division of Reed International Books
Australia Pty Ltd. All rights reserved.

© Reed International Books Australia Pty Ltd 2001
Logo design © 2004 by ETA/Cuisenaire®

Text by Marg McAlister
Edited by Gwenda Smyth
Designed by Karen Young
Illustrated by Melissa Webb

No part of this publication may be reproduced, stored in a
retrieval system, or transmitted, in any form or by any means,
electronic, mechanical, photocopying, recording, or otherwise,
without the prior written permission of the publisher.

Printed in Hong Kong by H & Y Printing Limited

04 05 06 07 08 09 10 11 12 13   10 9 8 7 6 5 4 3 2 1

CONTENTS

CHAPTER 1
School Records Day   1

CHAPTER 2
Sam's Winning Collection   8

CHAPTER 3
What Now?   16

CHAPTER 4
A Sweeter Collection   21

CHAPTER 5
Sabotage!   27

CHAPTER 6
More Sabotage   35

CHAPTER 7
Things Get Worse   42

CHAPTER 8
Mystery Solved   50

CHAPTER 9
The Winners   56

EPILOGUE   60

SCHOOL RECORDS DAY

Tom proudly held out the box. Sam and the others peered into it. It was half full of fingernail and toenail clippings.

"Yuck," said Yasmin. She backed away. "Half of them are dirty. They're disgusting!"

Tom grinned. He shook the box under her nose. "Bet I win!"

"You're sick."

Tom looked pleased at that. "Yep. My mom says that, too."

Their teacher, Mr. Hart, came crashing into the room. He slammed an armload of books onto his desk. "Okay. Sit down. Time to report on your World Records attempts." He pulled out his chair with a screech and sat down.

Mr. Hart never went anywhere quietly. The class had told him he could win the "noisiest teacher" prize.

Tom held up his box. "Here it is. 'Most Unusual Collection'—the winner! Over two hundred fingernail and toenail clippings. I counted them this morning."

"You could cheat with those," said Giorgio, looking put out. "It's easy to cut a toenail clipping into two. Then you could call it two toenail clippings."

Mr. Hart sighed. "Giorgio, it doesn't matter. It's for the most unusual collection. Tom could have six toenail clippings, or a thousand and six."

He swung around and pointed to the whiteboard. There was a big chart drawn on it. At the top it said Sun Valley School Records Day. "Anyone got anything to update?"

They all looked at the chart. Tom's name was under "Most Unusual Collection." The other categories were "Biggest," "Longest," "Fastest," "Tallest," "Biggest Collection," and "Endurance."

Yasmin put up her hand. "I have."

Half the class rolled their eyes. Yasmin put up her hand every day. She was building

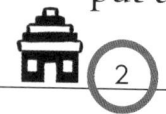

the world's biggest Lego village. At least, that's what she said. It was in her garage.

"Yes, Yasmin?" Mr. Hart stood up. He rubbed out the numbers next to Yasmin's name. "How big is it now?"

"Four yards by four point six yards," she said. "There are thirty-seven buildings. The biggest one is sixty-seven inches high."

"I haven't got room to write all that," said Mr. Hart. He wrote "14 x 15 ft" next to her name. "Very good, Yasmin. I can see you're going to be an architect." He looked around. "Anyone else?"

"I took a picture," said Yasmin. She waved a sheet of paper. "With my digital camera. I printed it out." She jumped out of her seat and gave the photo to Mr. Hart. Yasmin wanted to be famous.

"Thanks, Yasmin." Mr. Hart took the photo and put it on his desk. He didn't look at it. "Great work. Anyone else?"

Yasmin kept going. "My dad is getting angry. He says he wants his garage back."

"She's right," Sam whispered to Tom. "I heard him shouting this morning. His new car got dents in it last night. It was out in the hailstorm."

"Well, Yasmin, in two weeks it'll all be over," said Mr. Hart. "Now—ANYONE ELSE?"

"Yes," said Giorgio. "I have 108 different rocks in my collection now." He didn't sound very excited. He could see the number next to Sam's name under "Biggest Collection." It was 932. Everyone expected Sam to win.

Mr. Hart changed Giorgio's number from 103 to 108.

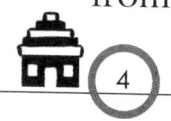

"Sam? Have you added any more toy cars to your collection?"

"No." Sam felt a bit guilty. Most of the others had been collecting for only about six weeks. He had started his toy car collection when he was two. People had given him cars for years. Every birthday. Every Christmas. They still did, even though he was too old to play with them now. His collection had been easy.

HOT COMPETITION

"Okay." Mr. Hart looked at the "Endurance" column. "Anyone beaten Vanessa's record for longest time playing a video game? No? How about most laps in the swimming pool...? Does Kim still hold the record?... Okay." He put down his black pen. "Remember, two weeks from today is awards day. Some of you will have to finish two days before that for judging. If you want to set an endurance record, you have to have witnesses. Any questions?"

Yasmin put up her hand again. "If I build a Lego cow, does that count as a building?"

Everyone looked at her. Mr. Hart seemed a bit glassy-eyed. "Does a cow count as a building?" he repeated.

Behind Sam, Tom snorted. Then Giorgio laughed. In seconds, the whole class was giggling.

Yasmin looked offended. "Well, it's made of Lego blocks, isn't it? And it's a separate thing. I have to count all the buildings. The things made of Legos."

Mr. Hart tried to stop laughing. His lips still curved up. "I don't know, Yasmin. I'll have to check that." He stood up. Some of the books on his desk crashed to the floor. At the front of the room, Maria dived out of her seat to pick them up.

"Thanks, Maria," said Mr. Hart. "Okay, that's all for World Records for today. Tom, put that box of clippings away. All of you, good luck with your records. The next update is Wednesday morning. Who's going to win?"

SAM'S WINNING COLLECTION

Sam looked at his toy car collection. Nine hundred thirty-two cars took up quite a bit of space. He had lined them up along the driveway. It looked like the world's biggest parking lot. He'd need a truck to get them to school.

That reminded him. It was nearly time for his Uncle Darrell to arrive. He was bringing his big concrete truck. Today was the day to pour the concrete for Dad's new garage. Sam had to get his cars off the driveway. If he didn't, Mom would be mad at him again.

Carefully, Sam started packing his collection back into the boxes. Trucks in one box. Family cars in another. Vans in here, racing cars in there...

The back door slid open. "Sam!" yelled his sister, Kimmy. "Can you come and help me measure this?"

SAM'S WINNING COLLECTION

He looked up. Kimmy stood at the back door. She was holding her knitting. Miles and miles of knitting. She looked tired. She looked cranky, too. Kimmy was going a bit nuts over this "longest scarf" thing. Early in the morning: knit, knit, knit. In her lunch hour: knit, knit, knit. Right up until bedtime: knit, knit, knit...

"In a minute," he said. "I have to pack these away. Uncle Darrell will be here soon." He moved on to the final row of cars and filled the last box. Then he dragged all the boxes off the driveway. "Why don't you bring the scarf out here? Then we can lay it out flat."

HOT COMPETITION

Kimmy looked horrified. "No way! It'll get all dirty!"

Sam looked at the perfectly clean driveway. "No it won't."

"It will! We have to do it inside."

Sam gave up. He went inside. They laid out the scarf along the hallway. Sam held it flat while Kimmy measured. She didn't let Sam do the measuring. Kimmy didn't trust anyone but herself. A silver thread marked off every yard. That was Sam's idea. It was supposed to save them measuring it from the start every time, but Kimmy still did it anyway. She was obsessed.

"Twenty-six point three eight yards!" Kimmy smiled. "That is thirty-seven inches longer than yesterday."

"Great," said Sam. "Now all you have to do is find a giant to wear it. Or you could share it among twenty people. Snip, snip…" He made cutting motions with his fingers.

"Ha, ha," said Kimmy. "You are soooo funny, I don't think." She stopped and listened. "Uncle Darrell's here!"

Beside them, the door of Lucas's room flew open. Their older brother shot out. "Hey, is that Uncle D—aaagggh!" He let out a shriek as he caught his toe on the edge of the scarf. He slammed into the opposite wall, putting out a hand to save himself.

"Owww!" He grabbed his wrist and howled. "Not again! That scarf is going to kill me!"

"Nobody else falls over it as often as you," said Kimmy. She quickly got out of reach and rolled up the scarf. Then she stuffed it in a backpack.

Lucas glared at her. "You trip me up in the kitchen. You trip me up in the family room. Now I can't even come out of my own bedroom."

"You should watch where you're going," Kimmy snapped. She threw the backpack into her bedroom. "I'm going to watch them pour the concrete."

They all ran out the front door. Uncle Darrell was backing his truck up the driveway. It was making a lot of noise. He was hanging out of the window, frowning.

"Watch the side of the house!" called Sam's mother.

"Okay, okay! It's cool!" Uncle Darrell steered the truck away from the house a bit. He hadn't been working for the concrete people very long.

Sam grinned at Lucas. "He'd better not hit the house," he said. "Mom will chase him out of town."

Kimmy squealed. "I think he's going to hit the side fence instead! Oh no!"

There was a grating noise. Then a lot of snapping and cracking. The fence tipped sideways. The three of them watched in horror.

Sam suddenly went pale. His car collection! He'd moved them from the driveway... to a place where they'd be "safe." Right near the fence.

"My cars! UNCLE DARRELL!" Sam ran back through the house and out the back door. Kimmy raced after him. They both stopped and stared.

The concrete truck was moving forward again, off the broken fence. Sam's mother had her hands over her mouth. His father was shouting at Uncle Darrell. Their neighbor was running out of his house.

Slowly, the truck rolled forward. Right back over the top of Sam's squashed boxes of cars. It flattened them some more. Then it stopped.

"Oh no!" Sam raced to what was left. "He ran over them twice!"

HOT COMPETITION

"Oh no, Sam." His mother looked stunned. "Oh, Sam…the fence…and your cars…Oh dear, I told you to put them away…"

"I did! I moved them off the driveway! How was I to know he didn't know how to drive the truck?" Sam bent down. He pulled back the torn cardboard. He picked out one car. It was very flat. The tires were all sticking out at funny angles. The others looked pretty much the same. Sam threw the car back on top of the box.

"Matey…" said Uncle Darrell, jumping out of the truck. "Gosh, I'm sorry…" He looked at Sam's mom. "Lauren, sorry about the fence…"

Sam turned away. He walked back into the house. Behind him were a lot of loud voices. He could hear his mother calling his name.

He went into his room and closed the door. Okay, toy cars were for little kids. His friends would think it was nothing. But he'd been collecting them all his life. They were kind of special.

He didn't really care about the record. But he did care about the cars.

WHAT NOW?

The next day, Sam sat down to think. His car collection was now just scrap metal. Their teacher said everyone had to have a go at a record. So he had to think of something else.

His uncle had said sorry about a million times. He said he was going to replace all the cars. Sam didn't see how he could do that. For years and years, Sam had been getting them. Some were even from overseas.

He tried to stop thinking about his cars. No cars... so how else could he set a record?

Some of the other kids were seeing how many levels of a computer game they could play. Others were seeing how long they could play computer games nonstop. They said that was way more fun than his toy cars.

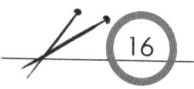

WHAT NOW?

What could he do that would be fun? And easy? What wouldn't take a long time to collect? Or to do? Not a giant Lego village, like Yasmin. Not a scarf, like Kimmy—never!

Sam went into the TV room. Kimmy was sitting there, staring at her knitting. Her needles clacked. She looked bored.

"I don't know how you can do that," he said. "Just knit all day long."

"At least I'm working at it," she said crossly. "Not like you and your cars. You don't have to do anything. It isn't fair."

"Well, they're gone now," Sam pointed out. He looked at Kimmy's knitting. She was right. He had told himself the same thing. It was too easy to collect cars. But he didn't know what else he could do.

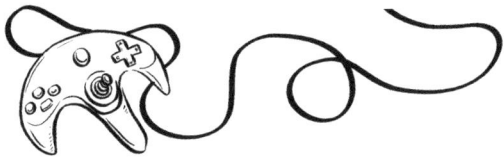

He spotted Lucas's Nintendo. "Maybe I could set a record in playing a video game," he said. "See how long I can stay awake."

"Nah," said Kimmy. "You'll end up crying."

She was right again. He had these funny eyes. Every time he played a video game for too long, his eyes got sore. Really sore. Then they started to water. Before too long he'd have tears running down his face. They weren't real tears—just sore eyes. But he looked kind of dumb, sitting there playing a game and crying.

WHAT NOW?

Sam left the room. It was a pain having a sister who was right all the time. As well as cranky all the time. He went and got his class list of things to do to set a record. There had to be something there.

"A collection," Sam said out loud. That was still the easiest thing. But collect what? It was getting too late to collect something else like, say, magnets. Anyway, they cost too much. He needed something cheap.

He read through the list. Someone in the *Guinness Book of Records* had collected gum wrappers. He'd put them together in a chain. That would be easy. But this guy had been doing it half his life. Sam didn't have half his life. He had just under two weeks.

Someone else had collected potato chip packets. Sam thought some more. Maybe lollipop wrappers? Aha! Sam sat up. Lollipop wrappers! Yes! They didn't eat lots of sweets in his house. But that didn't matter. He could go to shops. He could look in the bins for wrappers people had thrown away. His nose wrinkled. Mom would hate the idea of him raiding trash cans. Well, she didn't have to know.

Sam left the house. Lucky today was Sunday. He could ride his bike to lots of stores. Lots of trash cans. One collection of lollipop wrappers coming up...

A SWEETER COLLECTION

4

By the next Wednesday, Sam was sick to death of trash cans. He rode his bike home the long way. He went to six different stores. Six different trash cans. Tom went with him. At the last stop he said, "You should have collected toenails like me. That's easy."

"Don't be dumb, Tom," said Sam grumpily. "If I collected toenail clippings too, then you couldn't win, could you? There would be two 'unusual' collections. Both the same. How unusual is that?"

"Oh yeah," said Tom. "Didn't think of that." He looked at Sam's handful of sticky wrappers. "Yuck! They're all dirty."

"I'm going to wash them," said Sam. He stashed the latest ones in his bag. "Come on. You can help me. Since you have nothing to do."

HOT COMPETITION

They rode back to Sam's house. The minute they got there, his mother appeared at the back door. "Sam! Get yourself in here!"

"Uh oh," said Tom. "Maybe I'd better go home?"

"Coward. Stay here!" hissed Sam. He looked at his mother. "What's wrong, Mom?"

"I'll show you what's wrong." His mother looked almost as mad as when the fence got run over. She stomped off in front of him. Thump, thump, thump through the kitchen. Thump, thump, thump past Kimmy, knitting madly. Into the hallway. She stopped in front of his room and flung open the door. "What is that?"

Sam looked. Tom peered over his shoulder. "That" was his lollipop wrapper collection. Six shopping bags full. Okay, it looked like trash, but it wasn't really. Maybe it was the flies buzzing around it that made his mother mad.

"It's my collection," he said. "Lollipop wrappers. It's not rubbish."

"I know that," she said in a high voice. "Now take a closer look."

He went in. He was still half a room away when he saw why she was so mad.

"Oh," he said. "Ants."

"Ants and flies," said his mother. "This is too much, Sam. TOO MUCH. Get rid of them!"

HOT COMPETITION

She turned and stalked away.

Tom was making odd snuffling noises. Sam knew he was trying not to laugh. He wouldn't dare. He was a bit scared of Sam's mother. When she was in a temper, that is.

"Shut up and help," Sam said. "It wasn't my fault someone left the window open. I didn't let the flies in. Or the ants."

He went to the kitchen and got a giant trash bag. They tipped all the lollipop wrappers inside it. Then he got the bug spray. Zsssst. Zsssst. No more ants. No more flies. Well, there were bodies, but he got rid of those.

"See, it wasn't that big a deal," he told Tom. "Now to the bathroom. We have to wash these."

"You have got to be joking," said Tom. "Wash all those wrappers?"

"Are you my friend or what?"

"Okay, okay," said Tom. "Toenail clippings are much easier." Groaning, he followed Sam into the bathroom.

"Shampoo should do it," said Sam. "Lots of it. Mom has a big bottle. We'll use hers." He squirted half the bottle into the bath. Froth bubbled up. Mountains and mountains of it.

"Hmmm... do you think you used too much?" asked Tom. He stood back and watched while Sam tipped the wrappers into the bath. Lots of ants went in with them. The wrappers sat on top of the foam. Sam frowned. He stuck in his hand and stirred them into the water. Ants ran up his arm.

HOT COMPETITION

"Oh, gross," said Sam, brushing off ants. "Let's leave them to soak. We can't wash every single wrapper."

From out in the family room there was a thump and a yell. Sam grinned at Tom. "There goes Lucas, falling over Kimmy's scarf again."

They heard Lucas's raised voice. "You leave it there on purpose to trip me up!"

"I do not!" came Kimmy's voice in reply. "You never watch where you're walking!"

They heard her mother's voice join in. "What NOW? Listen, I am sick of these school records. Do you hear? Sick, sick, sick! What with cars and scarves and ants and flies…"

"Come on," whispered Sam. "Time to get out of here." He and Tom crept out of the bathroom and out the front door.

SABOTAGE!

Sam was in big trouble—again. His mom's shampoo had cost heaps, she told him. She had bought a big bottle to save money. Now most of it was gone.

As for the wrappers, they had been a soggy mess. Most were stuck together. After all his work, he'd had to throw them out.

Now what? All of Thursday he thought about it. Then all of Friday. By Saturday, he was ready to give up. He sat in his room looking at his toenails. Why couldn't he have thought of toenail clippings before Tom did?

The door banged open. Kimmy stood there, looking wild-eyed. "Have you seen my scarf?"

"It's in your backpack."

"I know that!" she screeched. "Have you seen my backpack?"

"No," Sam said. "Ask Lucas. He's the one who keeps falling over it. Maybe he's put it up on the roof or something."

Kimmy disappeared, bellowing for Lucas. Then he heard his mother's voice. "Kimmy, stop that yelling. Lucas is away at a camp, remember? He won't be back until Tuesday. Come on, I'll help you find it."

They searched everywhere, even on the roof—but the backpack wasn't there. Tom and three of Kimmy's friends arrived. They searched, too. The backpack was nowhere to be found.

"Someone's stolen it!" Kimmy threw herself on the sofa in despair. "All that work! Now it's gone!" She burst into tears.

Sam felt sorry for her. He knew how she must feel. A bit like he had felt when his cars were squashed. Or his lollipop wrappers had to be thrown out. But Kimmy had worked much harder than he had.

"Now, Kimmy. No one would have stolen it." Her mother hugged her. "Are you sure you didn't leave it at a friend's house?"

HOT COMPETITION

Kimmy just shook her head and kept sobbing.

"When did you last see it?"

"Yesterday," replied Kimmy in a watery-sounding voice. "At Yasmin's house. She was building her Lego village. I w-was knitting. Then I came home. With m-my backpack."

"Sam, go and see Yasmin," his mother said. "Just to make sure."

Sam and Tom left. Yasmin's house was only half a block away. The door at the side of the garage was open. Yasmin's father was in the driveway, washing the car. It had dents all over it.

"Wow," said Tom. "Is that from the hailstorm?"

"Yes," said Yasmin's dad, looking angry. "It is. Because there is no room in the garage. My new car is ruined. The Lego village stays nice and dry!" He scowled and ran his fingers over the roof.

"Uh—is Yasmin here?" asked Sam.

Mr. Riyad snorted. "Yes, she is here. Building, always building. In *my* garage."

SABOTAGE!

They walked up to the door. Yasmin was balanced on a chair. She was putting more Lego blocks on a tall building.

Sam looked around in amazement. There was hardly any room to move. The Lego village took up every bit of space. Buildings. Trees. Animals. Cars. People. All made of Lego.

"Wow!" he said. "This is terrific. Is anyone helping you?"

"No," said Yasmin proudly. "No one is allowed to. I said I'd build it all by myself. Isn't it great?"

"You must have been working on it all day. Every day." Tom bent over to look at a row of houses. He bumped a tall building beside them. It rocked a bit, then stood still.

Yasmin's mouth opened in horror. "Watch what you're doing! If any of this gets knocked over, I'll never fix it in time."

HOT COMPETITION

"You've got until next Wednesday," Tom said. "One building wouldn't take that long."

"But I've got lots more to do." Yasmin climbed down from the chair. "I'm going to set the school record with this. Probably the city record. Then I'm going to go for the world record." She grinned. "I've got someone from the newspaper coming next Wednesday when it's all finished."

"If your dad doesn't knock it over first," said Tom. "He doesn't look too happy."

Yasmin shrugged. "Well, I didn't bring the hail! He liked my village until then. He'll be happy again when he sees it in the paper."

Sam was a bit irritated. Yasmin was so sure she was going to win. What if someone else had built something bigger?

"We're here about Kimmy's scarf," he said. "Her backpack's missing. She had it here yesterday. Have you seen it?"

"No," said Yasmin. "She took it home with her." She laughed. "How could she lose her stupid scarf? She could hardly carry it, it was so heavy." She picked up some more Lego blocks. "I think I'll make a new skyscraper. There's no room for anything else."

"Well, see you," said Sam, stepping back carefully. "We have to keep looking."

"See you." Yasmin opened a box of Legos she'd found in a second-hand store. "By Monday, I'll have more new buildings!"

Sam and Tom left. They didn't know where else to look. Kimmy said she had come home with her bag. She was positive. She had dropped it on the back porch. Then she had gone shopping with her friends.

"It sure looks like it was stolen," said Tom. "Unless a dog dragged it away. Have you seen any dogs around?"

"No. Anyway, why would a dog take it? It had a scarf in it, not meat." Sam was stumped. Had someone taken it? And if so—who?

More Sabotage

6

By Monday morning the school was abuzz.

On Sunday afternoon Giorgio had checked his rock collection. Fifteen of the best rocks were missing. Then on Sunday night someone let Yasmin's dog into her garage. Seven of the buildings had been knocked down before she got it out.

"It was probably her father," Sam muttered. "He seemed pretty sick of it!" Yasmin heard him. She turned around. "It was not my father!" she yelled. "I bet it was you!"

Sam was shocked. "Why would I do a thing like that?"

"You were asking me about Kimmy's bag. This is payback." Then Yasmin stabbed a finger at Tom. "Or maybe it was you! On Saturday you said my dad might knock it all over. You're just trying to put the blame on him!"

"I am not!" Tom glared at her.

Sam looked around. Several of the other kids were looking at them. Some of them even looked suspicious! Sam couldn't believe it. Surely they didn't agree with Yasmin? Why would he and Tom do this?

"Come on," said Sam. "This is stupid. Of course we didn't do it."

"You're just jealous," Yasmin said. "First your cars got run over. Then your silly lollipop wrappers stuck together. Just because you can't win, you don't want anyone else to. I bet you stole your own sister's bag, then did this to me and Giorgio!"

"I did *not*!" Sam shook his head. There was a lot of muttering going on. He could see that some of the kids believed Yasmin. Giorgio especially. He had shown Sam his best rocks the day before they went missing.

"Come on, Tom. Let's get out of here." He walked away. Tom trotted after him.

"Can you believe them?" complained Tom. "As if we'd do that!"

"I know." Sam's heart was beating fast. The problem was, some of them did believe it. They knew Sam's chances at a record were gone. He was the most likely suspect. He didn't really believe Yasmin's father had let the dog in. Even if he had, what about Giorgio's rocks? That wasn't Yasmin's dad. Someone was behind all this.

"You realize we'll have to find out who it was," Sam told Tom. "It's the only way to prove it couldn't have been us."

"Oh, yeah? And how are we supposed to do that?"

"We'll just have to ask questions. And figure out who was around when things disappeared."

They worked out a plan. It was just a matter of logic, Sam decided. Logic and keeping your ears open. He explained it to Tom. "See, we know it's not us. Your collection is different from Kimmy's and the others. It's in a different section."

"Well, I know it's not me," agreed Tom. "How do I know it's not you? They were right. You're not doing too well." Seeing Sam's frown, he winked. "Just kidding."

MORE SABOTAGE

"You'd better be," said Sam. "I wouldn't take Kimmy's scarf, even if she is a pain. She's worked too hard on it. And she's not a suspect, either. She wouldn't take her own stuff."

"It's sure not Yasmin," said Tom. "There's no way she'd ever wreck that village."

Some music started to play through the loudspeakers. It was time for school to start.

"Okay," said Sam. "Keep your ears open today. We'll meet at my place after school. There's got to be a way we can solve this."

HOT COMPETITION

That afternoon they looked at their list of suspects. On the "innocent" list they had six names: Sam, Tom, Kimmy, Yasmin, Giorgio, and Yasmin's dad. They started an "unsure" list, but that got too long. In the end, it was easier just to make a "suspects" list. On that went the names of Giorgio's, Kimmy's, and Yasmin's friends. After all, who else could go into their houses or yards? Someone would have noticed a stranger.

"I still don't think any of Kimmy's friends would do this," said Sam. "Her three best friends have all entered different sections. Sarah has a collection of fruit stickers. Emily is going for the highest score in *Planet Raiders*. And Angela is making the smallest dollhouse. That's the opposite of Yasmin and Kimmy."

Tom shrugged. "Well, I don't know then. Who else could come here? You'd notice a stranger."

MORE SABOTAGE

"Only family," said Sam. "Uncle Darrell wouldn't do it. And Lucas has been away at camp since last Friday afternoon. He couldn't have taken Giorgio's rocks. Or put the dog in Yasmin's garage."

This was harder than it seemed. They were just going around in circles. In the end, Sam threw his pen down in disgust. "I give up. It must have been the invisible man." His head hurt from trying to think. "We'll just have to ask more questions at school tomorrow. Maybe something will come up."

7 Things Get Worse

At Sam's house, things got worse. Kimmy wasn't talking to anyone. On Monday night, she shut herself in her room and went to bed early. On Tuesday morning, her mother had to call her three times. Kimmy came out of her room with dark circles under her red eyes.

"Kimmy, you'll have to get over this," said her father. "It's only a scarf. I know you worked hard on it, but —"

Kimmy burst into tears again. "What do you know? It's not 'only a scarf'! Everything's just terrible."

"Oh, Kimmy," said her mother. "What can we do to help? How about if you keep knitting? Then if we find your backpack, we can just join the new bit on."

Kimmy just shook her head. She picked at a piece of toast for breakfast.

Then she went back to her room. They all looked at each other. They had never seen her like this before.

"If she doesn't get better, I'm taking her to the doctor," her mother said. "Oh, if only I could get my hands on whoever took her bag!"

"I wish I could, too," said Sam. "Half the kids think it was me or Tom. We're trying to find out who it really was." He hadn't slept much more than his sister.

HOT COMPETITION

It wasn't any fun being the prime suspect. Today Sam simply had to find out more.

At school, things got worse. Giorgio seemed to have joined forces with Yasmin. He cast dirty looks at Sam and whispered a lot. Finally, Sam couldn't stand it any longer. He went up to Giorgio.

"Come on, Giorgio. You don't really think I took those rocks?"

THINGS GET WORSE

Giorgio looked angry. "The last time I had them was Saturday afternoon, at your place. Then you helped me pack them in the cart to take them home."

"That doesn't mean I took them." Sam couldn't believe it. After Tom, Giorgio was his next best friend.

"Yeah, but when I got home it was getting dark. I put them in our garage. I locked it up. The next day, I sorted through them again. All the good ones were gone." Giorgio stared at him. "It had to be you!"

This was worse than Sam had thought. One of Giorgio's family must have opened up the garage again. Someone else must have been able to get in. He said so.

"No way. I checked with all of them." Giorgio turned his back and walked away. So did some of the others.

At lunchtime, Sam and Tom were called to the principal's office. He didn't say they had done it. But he did ask lots of questions. All they could do was say no, it hadn't been them.

HOT COMPETITION

Sam couldn't wait to get home, away from all those accusing eyes. When he did, there was another surprise waiting for him.

Lucas was home from camp. His sleeping bag and backpack were on the back porch. But that wasn't the surprise. Kimmy's missing backpack was there, too!

Sam's mouth fell open. Was this what had happened to the scarf? It had been taken to camp by mistake. This changed everything! He ran inside.

Lucas was sitting at the kitchen table. He had that look you get when you're in heaps of trouble. His mother was leaning against the sink. She looked mad.

THINGS GET WORSE

"Where was Kimmy's bag?" asked Sam. "Did you take it to the camp?"

Lucas shook his head. "It was a joke," he mumbled.

"Some joke." Sam's mother folded her arms. "Kimmy's been crying for days. And they've been saying Sam took it. Tell him what you did!"

Lucas sank down in his chair. "I only meant it as a joke," he said again. "I hid it under the house. I was going to use my teacher's cell phone on the bus to tell Kimmy where her scarf was… but I forgot." He looked miserable.

HOT COMPETITION

A shriek from outside told them Kimmy was home. She ran inside. "My backpack! Who found it?" Then she saw Lucas's face. She guessed right away. "Lucas! It was you! You took my bag to camp!"

Lucas had to tell his story again. "It was just payback," he said, looking at Kimmy, "because I was always falling over it. Just a harmless joke… I didn't mean it to be missing for more than an hour or two. I'm sorry."

Sam was puzzled. He thought Kimmy would be happy to get her scarf back. Or that she'd tell Lucas what she thought of him. But she didn't. She didn't smile, either. She just nodded and said, "Okay. But…" Then she sighed. "I'm not going in the competition now." With that, she went to her room.

Their mother shook her head. "I don't understand. I thought she'd be jumping for joy. What's wrong with her now?"

"Maybe she thinks someone else will get the record," said Sam. He knew there were other kids knitting scarves. Kimmy had lost four days. She could have been knitting all that time. Knitting the longest scarf ever recorded in the town.

But no. It was more than that. He just knew it.

Then it struck him. Maybe Kimmy was worried about him. And Tom. Because everyone thought they took Kimmy's bag—as well as Giorgio's rocks, and also let Yasmin's dog into the garage.

"I'll go and talk to her," Sam said.

8 MYSTERY SOLVED

Sam went to his sister's room and knocked. "Kimmy?"

"Go away," came her voice.

"Kimmy, please? Just for a minute."

"No." He heard her footsteps come to the door. She opened it a crack and peered at him. "I'm going out."

"But you just got here." He took a deep breath. "Are you worried about me and Tom?"

"Why?" She sounded shaky.

"Well, because everyone thinks we took your bag and we didn't. And we didn't do the other stuff either."

"I didn't think you did anything." She opened the door wider. There was a large bag hanging from her shoulder. "I know who did it."

"You do?" Sam was amazed. He'd never thought of Kimmy as a detective.

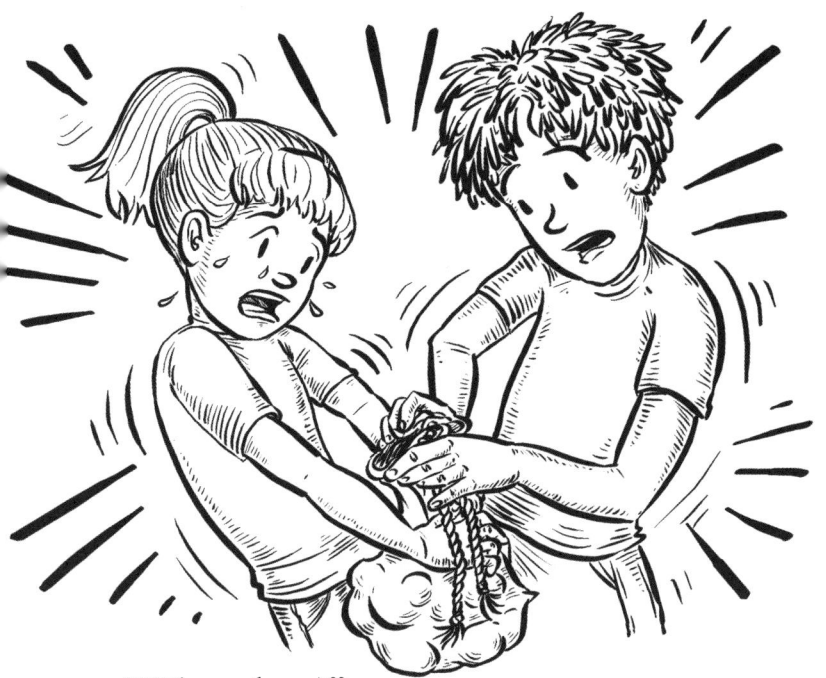

"Who, then?"

"I can't tell you. But I'm going to tell Yasmin and Giorgio who it was." She pushed past him. The shoulder bag made grating noises. Whatever was in there, it wasn't books.

Sam suddenly knew what it was. Rocks. Giorgio's missing rocks.

"Kimmy!" Sam grabbed the bag and opened the top. Yes. He was right. He stared at her. "It was you!"

Her eyes filled with tears. "Sssshh. I don't want Mom to know."

"But why?"

HOT COMPETITION

"Because I thought it was one of them who took my bag! Giorgio teases me all the time. He used to say nasty things. He made fun of my scarf and said he'd c-cut it up." Her voice shook.

"But Kimmy, I said that, too. And I was only joking. I bet he was, too."

"No. You don't know. He's never nasty when you're there." Tears spilled over. "I don't like Giorgio. He scares me. He's hidden my bag before. And he was here the day my scarf went missing."

Sam was stunned. "But what about Yasmin? Why did you let the dog in?"

Kimmy wiped her face on her sleeve. "She was like Giorgio. She only pretended to be friends. When I was there the other day, she said the scarf was stupid. She said my scarf wouldn't get in the newspaper. Her Lego village would. So I came home. Then my backpack was taken. And Y-Y-Yasmin's house is close… so I thought…"

MYSTERY SOLVED

Sam nodded. He and Tom would never have figured this out. Not one person, but two—Lucas and Kimmy. Both in his own family! But how could he fix this? How could Kimmy fix it?

"I'll come with you," he said. He was a bit mad at Giorgio. Kimmy didn't scare easily. If she was scared of Giorgio, he must have been nasty.

He went to tell his mother that he and Kimmy were going out. Then they set off to Yasmin's. Yasmin's dad's car was in the driveway. The side door to the garage was closed. They could hear music inside.

"She's in there," Sam said. "Come on."

They knocked once and went in. Yasmin was working on a Lego building. Her father was on the other side helping her. *Helping her?* thought Sam. He wasn't supposed to do that.

"Hey!" yelled Yasmin. "Knock, why don't you! You can't just walk in like that!"

"I did knock," said Sam. He looked at Yasmin's father. "I thought you had to do this all by yourself, Yasmin."

"She did do all the work herself," said her father. "The first time. Until the dog came in. I'm just helping her fix it." He glared at Sam. "I hear you are the one who let the dog in."

"No, it wasn't me," said Sam. "But I know who did. Yasmin, can we see you outside?"

Yasmin looked scared. She climbed off the chair and went outside with them. "You're not going to tell, are you? I really did do it all myself. But it got wrecked…" She looked as if she were going to cry.

MYSTERY SOLVED

Yasmin had worked hard on the village. Sam believed she had done it all herself. The first time, that is. So maybe if she and Kimmy worked out a deal... Sam told them what was on his mind. Yasmin had to fix up the rest herself. No more help from her dad. The village was already so big it had to win a prize, anyway. They wouldn't tell what they'd seen. And Yasmin couldn't tell anyone that Kimmy had let the dog in.

"Deal?" asked Sam.

"Deal," agreed Yasmin. She didn't look happy. But at least she agreed.

One down, one to go. They set off to Giorgio's.

9 THE WINNERS

Giorgio was happy to get his best rocks back. He wasn't happy with Kimmy at all. He said he'd tell everyone what she'd done. "I don't see why you should win a prize," he said. "You're a cheat. And a thief." He laughed. "At least now I'll win the biggest collection. Now that Sam's cars are out of it."

Sam looked at Kimmy. She was right about Giorgio. He really wasn't a very nice person. Not just because he was going to tell. He was just nasty about things. Why had he ever been friends with Giorgio?

"Fine," said Sam. "Do what you like. Kimmy's not going in the competition now anyway."

He walked away. "Come on, Kimmy. At least you don't have to worry about Giorgio anymore. He won't be coming to our place again."

They walked home together. For a long while Kimmy didn't say anything. Then, when they reached their house, she spoke. "I wish I hadn't done it. I felt bad all the time. Especially when they blamed you. I didn't know what to do. And my bag was still missing…"

"That's okay." Sam grinned at her. "How about Lucas hiding your bag! I reckon you can get him to do your chores for a month."

She gave a small smile. "I bet I could, too! But I won't. He's okay most of the time. And he got into heaps of trouble from Mom." She stopped and turned to look at Sam. "Giorgio's going to tell, you know."

"I know." He felt sorry for Kimmy. "Nothing we can do."

"So you know what? I'm going to tell them I let the dog in, too." Her voice sounded a bit wobbly. "I'm going to tell them everything. That Lucas hid the bag, and I thought it was Giorgio. Because he's so horrible. Or Yasmin, because of how mean she's been. Then I don't have to worry what they say."

Sam felt kind of proud of his sister. She was going to have a bad day at school. But she would do it.

"But I'm not going to tell about Yasmin's dad helping her. A deal's a deal. And he really didn't help her at the start." Kimmy took a deep breath. "All my friends will be here soon. I'll tell them first."

They went inside.

EPILOGUE

The Sun Valley School Records Day finally arrived. Kimmy didn't enter, and everyone knew why. Yasmin won the Biggest Lego Structure easily, of course. No one ever knew her dad helped her fix things. She got her photo in the paper, just as she had planned.

Giorgio didn't win the Biggest Collection. That went to Sam. He won it for the "Biggest Collection of Scrap Metal Toy Cars." His Uncle Darrell had entered the cars without telling him.

But the most popular prize of the day went to Mr. Hart. The kids invented a brand new Records section—the World's Noisiest Teacher. He won it hands down.